On Sabbath

Our Day of Rest

Don Harris

Think Red Ink Press
www.ThinkRedInk.com

On Sabbath

Our Day of Rest

Most people already have a view of Sabbath. Answer the following *true* or *false* questions to test your knowledge of the Sabbath Day:

(*True* or *False*)

1) We no longer *have* to keep any of the Commandments because we are now under grace. (p.6)

2) The Sabbath Commandment is less important than the others. (p.9)

3) We remember the Sabbath Day and keep it holy by remembering the spiritual rest Christ provided through redemption. (p.14)

4) If we do keep the Sabbath Day, we may keep it on any day we wish as long as it is one day in seven and we make that day holy. (p.18)

5) Jesus did not keep the Sabbath Day thereby providing an example to us all. (p.20)

6) Jesus taught that if we have an "ox in the ditch," we may work on the Sabbath. (p.23)

7) The Sabbath was changed from the seventh day to the first day of the week in honor of the resurrection. (p.24)

8) We have no way of knowing which day is the seventh day of the week because calendars have changed over time. (p.26)

9) Every day should be as a Sabbath Day to the Believer. (p.27)

10) The Sabbath is not re-affirmed (mentioned) as a New Testament Commandment. (p.29)

***

How did you do? Let's look at these questions one at a time:

1) We don't have to keep any of the Commandments because we are now under grace.
   FALSE

This is one of the most tenacious doctrines in Christendom. Paul tells us in the New Testament that we are no longer under the Law.

> *"Now we know that what things soever the law saith, it saith to them who are under the law:"* (Romans 3:19a)

> *"For sin shall not have dominion over you: for ye are not under the law, but under grace."* (Romans 6:14)

What does it mean to be *under the Law?*

The Apostle uses this term to describe our position before the advent of Christ. Before His coming, it would have been our *obligation* to justify ourselves before God by the works of the Law. He tells us that this would be an impossible task.

> Romans 3:20a, *"Therefore by the deeds of the law there shall no flesh be justified in his sight:"*

It is improper to try to gain justification by the Law because the Law **cannot provide justification**.

> Romans 3:20b, *"But now the righteousness of God without the law is manifested, being witnessed by the law and the prophets."*

We are to live by the Spirit and let the Law *witness* to our deeds. If we live by the Spirit, we will never violate the Law. If we violate the Law, we have not been true to the guidance of the Spirit. When we do live in this Spirit, we have righteousness imputed to us. It is, therefore, not called "our righteousness" but, more correctly, the "righteousness of God."

For example, if a man says he is following the Spirit inside himself as best he can, yet he continually finds himself in violation of the Eighth Commandment, *"Thou shalt not steal",* would you counsel him to continue in his "leading?" The Law does not *witness* to his leading. When his actions are held under the light of the Law, he is in violation; therefore, there is no witness to his deeds as good.

The inviolate actions of those led by the Spirit gain the witness of the Law and the Prophets. It should be easily agreed upon that we, as Spirit-led Believers, should never steal anything. If we steal, we lose the *witness* of the Law and frustrate the grace by which we are saved.

To further make the point, exchange the Eighth Commandment in the example above for the Seventh *("Thou shalt not commit adultery")* and see if you are willing to concede that this man is "led of the Spirit."

Exchange the Eighth Commandment for the Sixth Commandment (*"Thou shalt not kill"*) and think about it again. If a man told you that the Spirit of God is leading him in his everyday life and yet was found to commit adultery or murder, would you counsel this man to continue in his leadings?

It is obvious (even to those newest in Christ) that in using the Commandments as a guide, this man is not being led by the Spirit of God at all!

Do you agree? How did you make your determination? By the lack of the *witness* of the Law it is easy to see that this man is not being led by the Spirit. The lack of the *witness* of the Law and Prophets exposes unrighteousness no matter what source of "inspiration" we may claim.

The Law has not passed away. Indeed, it has only been rendered ineffectual to the *Spirit-led* Believer. However, we will find the Law still exists and is still in full force *IF* we step out of the Spirit's leadership and go our own way.

"But IF ye be led of the Spirit, ye are not under the law." (Galatians 5:18)

So, how can you know that you are not *under the law* and how can you know that you are *led of the Spirit?* Be led of the Spirit! The Law and the Prophets continually and clearly witness to your life and your deeds as **good** and **right**!

2) The Sabbath Commandment is less important than the others. *FALSE*

Many people have trouble placing the same emphasis on the Fourth Commandment as the others. If you insert the Fourth Commandment into the exercise mentioned above, and remain consistent in your thinking, it can become very difficult for you to ignore our God's Sabbath Day.

The *importance* of the Commandments is a curious consideration for it *presupposes* a central character – the one who is making the judgment. When pondering the importance of this Commandment, the articulate thinker will quickly ask, "Important to *whom*?"

In consideration of the importance of the Commandments, can we assume the *Author is* the central character and not us? Since we cannot assume authorship or editorial rights to the

Commandments, it is unfair (and unwise) to place any more importance on any *one* Commandment because it would force us to prioritize the Commandments of YHVH.

Let's look at how Jesus handled this situation when it was presented to Him:

> *"Then one of them, which was a lawyer, asked him a question, tempting him, and saying, Master, which is the great commandment in the law? Jesus said unto him, Thou shalt love the Lord thy God with all thy heart, and with all thy soul, and with all thy mind. This is the first and great commandment. And the second is like unto it, Thou shalt love thy neighbour as thyself. On these two commandments hang all the law and the prophets."* (Matthew 22:35-40)

Upon reading these words, some think Jesus was talking about some *new* Commandments; but, He was NOT. He was quoting the Law.

> *"And thou shalt love the LORD thy God with all thine heart, and with all thy soul, and with all thy might."*(Deuteronomy 6:5)

> *"Thou shalt not avenge, nor bear any grudge against the children of thy people, but thou shalt love thy neighbour as thyself: I am the LORD."* (Leviticus 19:18)

Isn't it interesting that Jesus did not choose from the list given to Him by the young lawyer trying to tempt Him? Rather, He chose from *outside* the Ten Commandments. It is clear that His attitude was that the Commandments should remain intact as well as free from qualifying or quantifying opinions:

> *"Think not that I am come to destroy the law, or the prophets: I am not come to destroy, but to fulfil. For verily I say unto you, Till heaven and earth pass, one jot or one tittle shall in no wise pass from the law, till all be fulfilled.* ***Whosoever therefore shall break one of these*** *least* ***commandments****, and shall teach men so, he shall be called the least in the kingdom of heaven: but whosoever shall do and teach them, the same shall be called great in the kingdom of heaven. For I say unto you, That except your righteousness shall exceed the righteousness of the scribes and Pharisees, ye shall in no case enter into the kingdom of heaven."* (Matthew 5:17-20 – Author's emphasis)

His usage of the term *"least Commandment"* is also very interesting. **Which would *YOU* call the least Commandment?**

When I ask for opinions about this, I am usually offered one of three responses; and, in the minds of most people, the Sabbath

Commandment is nearly always named as the least of the Commandments, followed by the fifth then the tenth, respectively:

> Exodus 20:12, *"Honour thy father and thy mother: that thy days may be long upon the land which the LORD thy God giveth thee."*

> Exodus 20:17, *"Thou shalt not covet thy neighbour's house, thou shalt not covet thy neighbour's wife, nor his manservant, nor his maidservant, nor his ox, nor his ass, nor any thing that is thy neighbour's."*

I am amazed at how different man's understanding is from Jehovah's. Men often reason that it is bad to steal, but they think nothing of *wanting something that belongs to someone else*. This is just like asking, "How could this be an important Commandment?"

This is a major point in Jesus' Sermon on the Mount. He goes into much detail to stress that there is a way to remain free from condemnation of the Law – by not living so close to it. He teaches us to "draw our borders" far from violating the Law so that we won't break it. To avoid adultery, He taught us to avoid lust. To avoid murder, we are to avoid hate. Though seemingly carrying less eternal consequences, dishonor shown to parents was the only sin punishable by death; therefore, this Commandment is obviously more important than other Commandments.

Furthermore, how could the Tenth Commandment possibly be a *least* Commandment when contained within it is the key to keeping them all?

You see, if we use reasoning to determine which of the Commandments is the most important, it only will lead to prioritization and, by necessity, the exaltation of one Commandment and the debasing of another will be the result.

The level of importance placed on the Commandments is not for us to decide. We are not authorized to decide. We are not capable of deciding.

You will quickly see that to place any Commandment in the category of "least" is a difficult task. Jesus knew this. He knew that to proclaim a "greatest Commandment" would specify the rest as lesser ones. **If Christ Himself would not touch this task, neither should we.**

> *"Whosoever therefore shall break one of these least commandments, and shall teach men so,* ***he shall be called the least in the kingdom of heaven****: but whosoever shall do and teach them, the same shall be called great in the kingdom of heaven."* (Matthew 5:19)

Who would want to be called "least" for all eternity? We are not to trifle with the Commandments of YHVH nor are we to attempt to rank or prioritize them.

3) We remember the Sabbath Day and keep it holy by remembering the spiritual rest Christ provided through redemption.
   FALSE

Have you ever noticed that the Commandments given at Sinai say little about *how* we are to accomplish them? One of the wonderful things about Messiah's ministry was that He not only taught what our God expects us to *do*, He said (to those having *"... ears to hear"*) **HOW** to accomplish this righteousness.

The Commandments themselves, however, say little about the logistics of obeying them – *with the exception of the Fourth Commandment!* Jehovah made this Commandment so plain that it is nothing short of outright rebellion to violate it. He devoted more space and more words to this Commandment than any other – nearly as many words as all the other Commandments combined! He explains this Commandment so thoroughly that it leaves no room for doubting *how* to carry it out.

He explains *what to do* and *who should do it.* He even includes *when, how, and why it is to be done*:

Exodus 20:8-11, *"Remember the sabbath day,* **(what to do)** *to keep it holy. Six days shalt thou* *labour, and do all thy work: But the seventh day* **(when to do it)** *is the sabbath of the LORD thy God: in it thou shalt not do any work,* **(how to do it)** *thou, nor thy son, nor thy daughter, thy manservant, nor thy maidservant, nor thy cattle, nor thy stranger that is within thy gates:* **(who should do it)** *For in six days the LORD made heaven and earth, the sea, and all that in them is, and rested the seventh day: wherefore the LORD blessed the sabbath day, and hallowed it."* **(why it is to be done)**

Although it is true that in Christ we have rest (and the Sabbath rest mentioned in Hebrews 4:9, *"There remaineth therefore a rest to the people of God"* is indeed speaking of that rest) we cannot let that Spiritual truth replace an act of obedience to the Law of YHVH. The technique of "spiritualizing" the Commandments is an old ploy used by those who do not want to keep the Commandments. They use this method to save themselves the trouble of actually making any uncomfortable changes in their lifestyle.

What if we apply this "spiritualization" technique to the other Commandments, as well? Can we spiritualize the Fifth Commandment by theorizing that the honor due to parents means only that we should hold *God, the Father* in high esteem? How can we argue against this idea? We can easily see the spiritual correlative between our earthly parents and our Heavenly Father. Using this method there is no need to honor any *actual* person or persons on the earth as long as we fulfill the Commandment in a "spiritual" sense.

Of course, this line of reasoning falls hard on the ear and causes turmoil in the heart – *because it is WRONG!* The parallel, however, does hold true. We *should* honor our heavenly Father and obey Him. The spiritual idea should *NOT REPLACE* the *acts* of obedience to our mother and father. It must not render the respect for our earthly parents as inconsequential. **Why should we forsake the lower and lesser physical obedience for the higher spiritual value?** If we do so, have we not abolished the Commandment?

What if I taught you that the Seventh Commandment (regarding adultery) imposes only a "spiritual morality" and pertains only to "spiritual fidelity"? What if I said that the adultery spoken of in the antiquated Law of yesteryear applies only to the *fidelity* of the Church to Christ; therefore, the "spiritualization" of the Law leaves us free to actually commit whoredom and adultery? By exchanging physical and outward obedience for the inward and spiritual truth I could easily make this erroneous argument.

Likewise, if we are careful not to profane the Holy name of God (Third Commandment) in some *spiritual* way, would that make us free to *verbally* use it any way we wish? **NONSENSE!**

None of these ideas even resemble good judgment; yet, many readily apply this convoluted theory to the Fourth Commandment without a qualm. Taking a strictly spiritual view of Sabbath weakens the argument for keeping it as YHVH intended. It provides us an excuse and bolsters our creaturely (natural) reluctance to keep any of His Commandments.

The viewpoint of Sabbath being an inward and spiritual reality can only be rightly held by those who are **wholly compliant to the Commandments** *outwardly*. Think about the credibility that you would give a Bible teacher who is guilty of unabashed adultery while he teaches on the spiritual aspects and applications of the Seventh Commandment. This is as ridiculous as someone teaching that keeping the Fourth Commandment is "taking comfort" and "resting in Christ's finished work of redemption", while at the same time living in flagrant violation of His Father's Seventh Day Sabbath!

The spiritual aspect of the Commandments is of great value. It cannot be ignored, nor should it be. To ignore the insight that the Holy Spirit has opened to us about the Laws and ordinances of the Old Testament would be to deny the most valuable asset of the new birth. As Believers, we cannot be complete without BOTH an understanding consideration of the spiritual AND obedience to the clear demands of the Commandments. We cannot justify ourselves by doing the physical Commandment-keeping, nor can we enjoy God's favor by neglecting the Spiritual aspect of His Commandments. It is not a matter of choosing BETWEEN the spiritual and physical; rather, it is a decision to choose BOTH.

Although there is a value to be found in the parallel of Christ's finished work, taking of relaxation and rest, the Sabbath can only be *remembered* and *kept holy* according to the Author's explicit instructions. These instructions are simple, "***REMEMBER*** *the Sabbath day* [in order to] ***KEEP IT HOLY.***"

4) If we do keep the Sabbath Day, we may keep it on any day we wish as long as it is one day in seven and we make that day holy.
FALSE

Once again the Commandment is clear that we are to remember ***THE*** Sabbath Day, not *A* Sabbath day. Too much language and too many words were used in this Commandment to get this wrong! If the Father's intent was to get us to rest one day in seven, the wording could have been like that in Leviticus 25:2-4, *"...A Sabbath,"* referring to a sabbatical year for the land to rest. There was no particular year for the land to rest, just one in seven, in order to facilitate crop and fallow field rotation.

The Almighty God said to remember *THE* Sabbath Day and keep it Holy. He did not say to *have a Sabbath* or *make a Sabbath.* He said to *REMEMBER* it. The Sabbath He wants us to keep by remembrance is the one that He blessed and sanctified. Only **the Sabbath Day of creation** can be *remembered.*

Let's look at the difference in *keeping* the Sabbath Day holy and *making* the Sabbath Day holy. It is only possible to *keep* and *remember* what has **already been done**. It is only possible to make or create what has yet to be done. If we *make* another day our Sabbath, we must also *make* it holy. Jehovah has already ordained and sanctified a particular day as the Sabbath and *He* has made it holy. It is our responsibility to *remember this day* and *keep it holy.*

The *seventh-day Sabbath* of creation is the only Sabbath that we can *remember* – and the only one that the Creator Himself made holy. Whether we ignore the Sabbath altogether or keep it on a different day, the *seventh-day Sabbath* is the *only* Sabbath that fits this Commandment without a myriad of mental calisthenics or the inclusion of extra-Scriptural authorities to justify.

There are some who may attempt to teach you that

the Sabbath was *rightfully* changed to the sun-day (the first day of the week); so, I challenge you to discover the truth about this supposed change for yourself. If you do encounter these folks, ask them this question, "If the Sabbath was changed, who changed it and why was it changed?"

In addition, the authority for changing from the seventh-day Sabbath to the sun-day must be questioned. I have traveled this road many times, and have found the answers to be a *less than honorable* reflection of religion's past. We will discuss some of my discoveries later. In the meantime, here is a thought…even if the Scriptures would concede to your desire of another day, just how do you plan to make holy [sanctify] the day that you choose?

5) Jesus did not keep the Sabbath Day thereby providing an example to us all.
FALSE

Although the accusation is often made, Jesus NEVER violated the Sabbath. He is completely innocent of this charge. Over the years the Pharisees and Scribes added (what Messiah called) "burdens" to the Law. These were added rules making it extremely difficult to live under Jehovah's Commandments. Many of these rules were a part of tradition (not the Law) and Jesus was constantly found in violation of them. The

Son of God considered these rules "burdens" that kept Him from His Father's work.

One day, Jesus and his disciples were found gathering corn. After rubbing off the kernels with their hands and eating it, the Pharisees asked Him why He did, "...that which is unlawful" on the Sabbath Day. He answered with a question, *"Why don't you question your patriarchs? Why don't you see the true heart of God and look into the past before you invent all these laws and traditions?"*

Then He said, *"But if ye had known what this meaneth, I will have mercy, and not sacrifice, ye would not have condemned the guiltless."* (Matthew 12:7) Look! Jesus was quoting from Hosea 6:6, *"For I desired mercy, and not sacrifice; and the knowledge of God more than burnt offerings."*

God desires us to have the knowledge of Him more than He desires offering, sacrifice, and even Commandment-keeping. We know David to be a man after God's own heart. He was keenly aware of the heart of God and what brings Him pleasure. Somehow he knew that the sanctified shewbread was available to him for food when he needed it. He took it, ate it, and even gave some to his men.

I have searched the Scriptures to no avail for David's reasons for doing this and have come to believe that he simply knew the heart of God. Of course, Jesus also knew this; and, if you know it then you will live in His Law and in His right order, too.

We are lost without the Holy Spirit to guide us. Remember, the Law is a Schoolmaster to bring us to Christ so that we might be justified by faith. Jesus, the Messiah, lived in this knowledge. My whole purpose in writing this essay is to compel you, dear reader, to know Him in all His fullness. Just as the Apostle said, *"That I may know him, and the power of his resurrection, and the fellowship of his sufferings... "* (Philippians 3:10)

The Pharisees knew the book. Jesus knew the Author. The Scribes knew the words. David knew *the Word.*

We should live in the Gospel Order -- not in contradiction to the Law, but in unison and harmony with **every letter of the Law**. We cannot do this by knowing the Law in the *"oldness of the letter."* We can only do this by having a direct and living relationship with the Author of it.

Jesus never violated His Father's Law. Obviously, His actions were misunderstood by "legalists" who made the rules harder than were necessary. We may well find that God's Law is easier to keep than we have been taught.

6) Jesus taught that if we have an "ox in the ditch," we may work on the Sabbath Day.
FALSE

The "ox in the ditch exemption" is quoted repeatedly as a valid reason for not keeping the Sabbath Day. By declaring "emergencies" many attempt to use this idea as an excuse to do almost anything on the Sabbath Day. Unfortunately, (for those who quote it) this has no basis in fact. The following is a list of the pertinent Scriptures:

> Luke 14:5, "*And answered them, saying, Which of YOU shall have an ass or an ox fallen into a pit, and will not straightway pull him out on the sabbath day?*"

> Luke 13:15, "*The Lord then answered him, and said, Thou hypocrite, doth not each one of YOU on the sabbath loose his ox or his ass from the stall, and lead him away to watering?*"

> Matthew 12:11, "*And he said unto them, What man shall there be among YOU, that shall have one sheep, and if it fall into a pit on the sabbath day, will he not lay hold on it, and lift it out?*"

Note the use of the pronoun "you" in each of these

instances. Jesus was showing the hypocrisy of the Pharisees. Their opinion was the subject of His remarks. Messiah was not saying it was permissible to pull an ox out of the ditch on the Sabbath Day. He was saying that these Pharisees demanded from others that which they were not willing to abide by themselves. These teachers of the Law evaluated an ox and a man – and the ox's life and well-being was deemed superior.

Let me say here that Christ was not necessarily saying that they were wrong for pulling out the ox or for leading the animal to water, nor was He giving overall license to break the Law for men's deemed "emergencies." Whatever the Lord speaks to you personally is between you and Him. **We must be careful adding to the Scriptures what simply is not there.** We must at least be as careful as the Son of God to not to make editorial decisions about the immutable Law of God.

7) The Sabbath was changed from the seventh day to the first day of the week in honor of the resurrection. *FALSE*

History reveals that the original sun-day worship was that of the sun god, Apollo. The Emperor Constantine was a worshiper of Apollo and incorporated many of the signs, symbols, and theology into the doctrine of what was then known to Rome as Christianity. Sometime, in the year 321

AD, he moved the day of worship from Sabbath (the seventh day of the week) to the sun-day (the first day of the week). Then he issued a law **prohibiting manual labor on the sun-day** while, at the same time, he ordered the playing of games and sports on the Sabbath Day.

> "He enjoined the observance, or rather forbade the public desecration of Sunday, not under the name of Sabbatum, but under its old astrological and heathen title, Dies Solis, familiar to all his subjects, so that the law was as applicable to the worshippers of Hercules, Apollo, and Mithras, as to the Christians. There is **no reference whatsoever in his law either to the fourth commandment or to the resurrection of Christ**." (My emphasis) (Book Source: The History of the Church)

The idea of sun-day worship coming about because of the resurrection is a little harder to track; still, there is NO Scriptural basis for it. As a matter of fact, there is no factual basis for the resurrection occurring on the sun-day at all.[1] The Scriptures tell us exactly when it occurred; but, this is nearly never taught. Nowhere to be found is there a reference to Jehovah setting aside another day for worship; and certainly He did not set a day

---

[1] For more information on the events of resurrection, order "Reconciling the Resurrection" at www.ThinkRedInk.com.

other than the seventh-day Sabbath for rest.

8) We have no way of knowing which day is the seventh day of the week because calendars have changed over time.
FALSE

While it is true that calendars have changed over time, the days of the week have never changed. For example, when the 46 BC Julian calendar was replaced by the Gregorian calendar in 1582, the order of the days remained the same. They subtracted ten days from the number of days in the month – NOT from the number of days in the week. This left the order of the days intact. (See below)

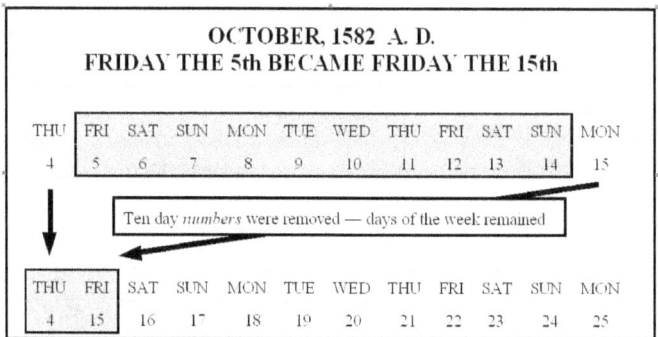

OCTOBER, 1582 A. D.
FRIDAY THE 5th BECAME FRIDAY THE 15th

THU	FRI	SAT	SUN	MON	TUE	WED	THU	FRI	SAT	SUN	MON
4	5	6	7	8	9	10	11	12	13	14	15

Ten day *numbers* were removed — days of the week remained

THU	FRI	SAT	SUN	MON	TUE	WED	THU	FRI	SAT	SUN	MON
4	15	16	17	18	19	20	21	22	23	24	25

The chronological experts are in agreement that the *order* of days is the same today as has been from the beginning of history. This became an academic argument when it was realized that the Jewish record and calendars record the days sequentially from early history. They don't accurately record back to the creation, but I understand they *do* go all the way back to the days in the wilderness when God fed the children of Israel manna. When the manna did **not fall on the Sabbath**, it clearly marked the seventh day. (I think it is safe to assume that God, since creation, knew which day was the seventh!)

We also have the more recent testimony of God's Son honoring the Sabbath and we can certainly assume He knew which day it was.

Using these calendars, we can project to the present day, and we can be assured that the Seventh Day (now called Saturday) has been and indeed still is the Sabbath Day.

9) Every day should be as a Sabbath Day to the Believer.
FALSE

Every day is *NOT* to be a Sabbath Day. The very definition of sanctification is "to set apart" or "set aside." Set apart? Set aside? From *what*?

Here we find yet another example of the spiritualization of a pure principle (see question #3 above). Yes, we are to live and enjoy the *"rest that remaineth to the people of God"* and this is life "in

Christ," but these things do not fulfill the Commandment. In order to fulfill the Commandments, we must accomplish their demands on us or we are "none of His." Jesus said, *"Think not that I am come to destroy the law, or the prophets: I am not come to destroy, but to fulfil."* (Matthew 5:17)

How did the Messiah fulfill the Commandments? By **keeping** them!

The Fourth Commandment makes it clear that we are to distinguish the other six days from the seventh. The statement, *"Six days thou shalt do all thy work"* is as much a part of the Commandment as the command to rest on the seventh day. *We cannot fulfill this Commandment by keeping a Sabbath every day*.

Many say, "We should worship everyday!" Such a statement indicates a lack of knowledge (to say the least) and wickedness (at worst). I say, unlearned, because the Commandment says nothing about *worshipping* at all. It is wickedness because its diversion from the truth further promotes lawless attitudes that affirm people in their wrongdoing.

It may sound very spiritual to say, "We should worship everyday," but it would be ludicrous to say that we should refrain from working every day. The Commandment is clear. We are to refrain from work on the Sabbath Day. The

Commandment says nothing about worship.

Some believe that there is Biblical evidence that the early Church worshipped on the first day of the week (supposedly proving a sun-day Sabbath); however, isn't it peculiar that there are no records that the disciples, apostles or any of the early church fathers were willing to work on the seventh day?

Of course, we may worship on any day we wish, but **this does not fulfill the Fourth Commandment**. This Commandment demands that no **work** be done on the Sabbath. If anyone is so deluded to think that if they worship every day they will fulfill the Fourth Commandment, it is likely because they have never actually read what this Commandment says.

10) The Sabbath is not re-affirmed (mentioned) as a New Testament Commandment.
FALSE

> Matthew 19:18-19, *"He saith unto him, Which? Jesus said, Thou shalt do no murder, Thou shalt not commit adultery, Thou shalt not steal, Thou shalt not bear false witness, Honour thy father and thy mother: and, Thou shalt love thy neighbour as thyself."*

Many of the Commandments are not mentioned in the New Testament account bearing these words of Christ found in the book of Matthew. For example, where can we find reiterated in the New Testament the Commandment forbidding the carving of images? Where is the Commandment found in these books forbidding other gods *"before"* Jehovah rewritten word for Word? When did Jesus ever say, *"Thou shalt not covet?"*

By no means should we condone covetousness or idolatry by the absence of these Commandments in written form; nor, should we dismiss any holy Commandment of Jehovah because it cannot be found printed within the New Testament's pages.

Of course, some may maintain that the *behavior* of the Apostles and followers of Christ is more than enough corroboration to affirm the continuance of a Commandment – and to this I would heartily agree! We can be assured that the Apostle John was still honoring the Commandment, *"Thou shalt have no other gods before me"* when we read his words, *"Little children, keep yourselves from idols."* (1 John 5:21) Furthermore, even though it is not recorded that the Lord Jesus ever made the statement, is there an apostolic writer who did not mention the sin of covetousness?

There are numerous models depicting the *philosophy* and *behavior* of the Disciples of Christ (including the writings of the Apostles) that affirm and re-affirm the Old Testament Commandments are applicable to the New Testament Believer. Even recorded history, both secular and religious, confirms that the first Believers set aside the Sabbath as a holy day.

There is yet a little known passage in the New Testament that stands as a **Scriptural example**, or re-affirmation of the Fourth Commandment and its adherence by those closest to the Savior.

> *"And that day was the preparation, and the Sabbath drew on. And the women also, which came with him from Galilee, followed after, and beheld the sepulchre, and how his body was laid. And they returned, and prepared spices and ointments; **and rested the Sabbath day according to the commandment**."*
> (Luke 23:54-56 Author's emphasis)

These women had spent the last three and one-half years[2] following the Messiah. They heard Him preach, teach, and minister. They heard Him debate the Law with the best of the best in the synagogues. Anyone who believes that the "New Testament Believer" is exempt from these legal

---

[2] The Scriptures do not specify the length of Messiah's ministry. It is commonly held that it was three and one-half years.

forms would have to ask why these women were compelled to honor an outdated and unnecessary Commandment. Why, after accompanying Christ on more than 182 Sabbath Days, after witnessing the day by day example of the Son of God Himself, would they be compelled to keep a Commandment that had been abolished by the Savior?

If the Scripture said only that they "...*rested the Sabbath day,*" we could surmise that perhaps they were keeping the Sabbath because it was an old habit or because they feared reprisal of the religious leaders; but, we can make no such assumption for the Scripture is clear.

Their refusal to do work was **"...*according to the Commandment.*"**

We can easily find recorded in Scripture the righteous acts of those who called Christ "Lord." These actions affirm the Commandments by *example;* but, when the *reason* is given for the behavior of these obedient women who were so close to our Savior during His lifetime, there is actually *more* proof for the re-affirmation of the Fourth Commandment than there is for the other nine Commandments!

***

PART TWO

More Points On Sabbath

The Sabbath has these exciting peculiarities:

1) The Sabbath was a part of the creation. (p.34)
2) The Sabbath was pre-Noahic covenant, pre-Abrahamic covenant, and pre-Law. (p.37)
3) The Sabbath was an integral part of the Law and many laws and holy days were based upon and constructed around Sabbath Days. (p.39)
4) Sabbath observance was included in the Ten Commandments. (p.40)
5) Sabbath-keeping is mentioned throughout the Old and New Testament Scriptures. (p.42)
6) Jesus mentioned the Sabbath as a factor at the consummation of the age. (p.44)
7) The Sabbath is clearly witnessed by both the Law and the Prophets. (p.45)
8) The Sabbath will be a part of time-keeping and worship in the Kingdom of God throughout eternity. (p.47)

Let's look at these peculiarities one at a time:

1) The Sabbath was a part of the creation.

The Bible says, "God *blessed and sanctified* the seventh day." Sometimes I think we miss important understanding because we don't pause to comprehend the words we read. To *bless and sanctify* simply means *to set apart*. God set the Sabbath Day apart from all the others.

Consider this poser:

• Did the Creator God *create* the Sabbath?

In order to answer, we must first consider whether God worked (created) on the seventh day and whether the world was made in six days or seven. (After all, Jesus said that the Sabbath was *MADE* for man.) Did YHVH create the Sabbath? The answer is *NO!* God did not *create* the Sabbath. He did not create the Sabbath Day any more that He created days eight, nine, or ten. He did *set it aside* and *blessed* it. The subsequent days came about as products of a galaxy already set into motion. Admittedly, they were set into motion by YHVH; however, they were not a part of the days of creation.

Some make the claim that the Sabbath was created on the seventh day. However, the Sabbath was not *created* – it was *set apart*. Had He *created* the Sabbath it would have been further work. God *made* it by setting it apart.

The seventh day was the first day, having all of its parts intact, that the world enjoyed. This wonderfully beautiful day was a product of God's planetary system and was the first of many more to come. As the first daylight of the completed creation dawned, it shone on all that God had made; and, from the Creator's pleasure in His creation, arose the first gift of God to mankind – the Sabbath Day – the first-fruit of His new world!

He decided to set this day apart from all the others; a day for man to remember his Creator. Creation itself brought about the Sabbath Day and God set it apart and gave it – as a gift – to us!

Seven days are the contents of one week. God's pattern of creation and rest was to be used by man as a pattern for his own activity. Look at the Fourth Commandment and notice how He reflects back to those days of creation:

Exodus 20:8-11, *"Remember the sabbath day, to keep it holy. Six days shalt thou labour, and do all thy work: But the seventh day is the sabbath of the LORD thy God: in it thou shalt not do any work ... For in six days the LORD made heaven and earth, the sea, and all that in them is, and*

*rested the seventh day: wherefore the LORD
blessed the sabbath day, and hallowed it."*

It is from the Fourth Commandment that we get
the basis for our seven-day week *and* the basis of
our work and rest cycle. Have you ever considered
that there is NO REASON WHATSOEVER for a
seven-day week except for the Bible's record of
creation? Why not a five or a ten-day week?
Consider that there is nothing in nature to indicate
that we are to rest on the seventh day. There are
no animals that cease their labor on this day. The
crops don't stop growing. There is nothing to
show us that we should keep this Commandment.
Simply, we must rest because our God said so!

> *"Why is one day more important than
> another, when all the daylight in the year is
> from the sun? By the Lord's wisdom they
> were distinguished, and he appointed the
> different seasons and festivals. Some days
> he exalted and hallowed, and some he
> made ordinary days."* (Sirach 33: 7-9 –
> Apocrypha NRSV)

The same creation record that declares that the
world will operate on a seven-day cycle also
declares the Sabbath to be an integral part of that
week. Modern-day science with its evolutional
theories makes every attempt to remove YHVH
from life's equation. The Sabbath serves as the
last vestigial sign of God as Creator in the earth.

The Sabbath was pre-Noahic covenant, pre-Abrahamic covenant, and pre-Law.

You may be surprised to find that the famous appearance of the Ten Commandments is historically not where Sabbath-keeping makes its debut. It actually happened in the wilderness just before the Commandments were given. It happened at the manna incident, and it was given to the children of Israel *as a test of obedience.* Read it again:

"Then said the LORD unto Moses, Behold, I will rain bread from heaven for you; and the people shall go out and gather a certain rate every day, that I may prove them, whether they will walk in my law, or no. And it shall come to pass, that on the sixth day they shall prepare that which they bring in; and it shall be twice as much as they gather daily. ... This is that which the LORD hath said, To morrow is the rest of the holy sabbath unto the LORD: bake that which ye will bake to day, and seethe that ye will seethe; and that which remaineth over lay up for you to be kept until the morning. ... And Moses said, Eat that to day; for to day is a sabbath unto the LORD: to day ye shall not find it in the field. Six days ye shall gather it; but on the seventh day, which is the sabbath, in it there shall be none. And it came to pass, that there went out some of the people on the seventh day for to gather, and they found none. And the LORD said unto

Moses, How long refuse ye to keep my commandments and my laws? See, for that the LORD hath given you the sabbath, therefore he giveth you on the sixth day the bread of two days; abide ye every man in his place, let no man go out of his place on the seventh day. So the people rested on the seventh day." (Exodus 16:4-30 – abridged)

Chronologically, the event in this passage occurred just *before* the Ten Commandments were given. (Exodus 20) The Father was feeding manna to His murmuring people in the wilderness. As is His way, He added a caveat – a right ordering or proviso – to pick up double food on the sixth day and not collect it at all on the Sabbath.

This Sabbath exercise was His "pop quiz" before the big test. That's why He said, *"...that I may **prove** them, whether they will walk in my law, or no."* His demands were not great or impossible. They weren't even difficult. All He asked was that they do things His way.

Unfortunately, the story ends with the failure of the people to do as their Creator commanded, and so we hear Him say, *"How long refuse ye to keep my commandments and my laws?"*

Jehovah wanted His people to stay *"in their place"* on the Sabbath. I believe this phrase is an obvious indication of inactivity. He said, *"To morrow is the rest of the holy sabbath unto the LORD: bake that which ye will bake to day, and seethe that ye will seethe; and that which remaineth over lay up for you to be kept until the morning."*

Isn't He plainly stating that we are to cook only what we will eat today and lay up (unprepared and in its original form) that which we will eat tomorrow? Preparation was expected; eating was expected; but, **gathering** certainly was forbidden.

I believe that the Sabbath continues even today to be a test of our obedience.

2) The Sabbath was an integral part of the Law and many laws and holy days were based upon and constructed around Sabbath Days.

Many Laws were based upon, and constructed around, the Sabbath Days. The Feasts and Holy Days of the Old Testament are replete with mentions and additions of Sabbath Days. Some Feast days could have up to three Sabbath Days *inside of one week's time*.

All Sabbaths have received certain distinctions. The *"Sabbaths and new moons"* spoken of in the statutes and ordinances, as well as in the New Testament, were altogether different from the weekly Sabbath. Before Yeshua came and fulfilled them in His exemplary life, they were to be observed and kept to the letter. Nevertheless, the calculation of and familiarity with Sabbath was an integral part of the Law; and without it obedience to the Law would have been impossible.

I submit that the Sabbath continues to be a part of the Law that our Father has *written in our hearts*. Without a working knowledge of the Sabbath, we will find our walk with Christ incomplete and ourselves less than obedient to the Guide within us.

3) Sabbath observance was included in the Ten Commandments.

Inclusion of Sabbath observance in the Ten Commandments is a clear point of its importance and creates a wholly different set of arguments for and against its practice in the life of a modern-day Believer. If it were not included in the Commandments, we might be more easily persuaded to believe it is of less moment or importance today.

Here is an opposing example. The wearing of phylacteries was commanded in the Scriptures; but, this command was not included in the Ten Commandments. If someone said that you were not living up to the pleasure of YHVH because you don't wear phylacteries, (or strings on the borders on your garment, or a beard because you are not to shave off its "corners") you could argue as to the pertinence of such a Commandment. But, if you were breaking one of the Ten Commandments, anyone would have a hard time seeing your action as obedient to the Spirit who originally wrote these Commandments and sent them forth.

Remember, we are talking about the *ONLY* document written with the finger of God! It is one of the only writings that contain God's words *purely*. It is inconsistent (to the point of hypocrisy) to preach and teach that the Bible is an immutable document if the words actually written by God Himself are changeable and impertinent!

The Almighty chose to include Sabbath observance as part of the Ten Commandments. He chose to write it in stone and enforce it for centuries. Who are we to say that Sabbath not for us today? Isn't it odd that more modern-day Believers are willing to embrace a book of their own era as the inspired, infallible, and immutable "Word of God" than are willing to accept the words *actually* written by our God – in stone – with His own finger?

4) Sabbath-keeping is mentioned throughout the Old and New Testament Scriptures.

The list of references that could be cited here would be extensive. Suffice it to say that the Sabbath was a practice of the true worshipers of the God of Abraham, Isaac and Jacob, and its existence is an uncontested fact for any Bible reader. However, does this relate as pertinent to the present-day worshiper? Was the Sabbath laid down or set aside in the days of Christ, or in the days of the Apostles, or at any time in the days of the early Church?

There is no evidence that the Sabbath was ever even considered for change until the Emperor Constantine changed it to conform to his own heathen custom of sun worship. Written accounts of his dubious "conversion" have left me wondering why anyone would believe that he was Christian or a friend of the Church.

Constantine single-handedly adulterated the pure faith of the Church into the superstitious magic act it resembles today in Catholicism. A study into this metamorphosis of the body of Christ by the Emperor should make one wonder what truth is left in this poor ravaged shell of the *"...faith once delivered to the saints."* We certainly will be hard-pressed to find any resemblance to the faith and practice witnessed in the New Testament.

We have all been sold a bill of valueless goods. Now, it is our duty to find the right path, forsaking all tradition and familiarity, and then to muster the courage to walk in the way shown to us! A jaundiced eye should be used in evaluating the old ways, doctrines, and traditions handed us by this nemesis church.

In addition to sun-day worship, look at a list of errors taught to us as truth: infant baptism, transubstantiation, purgatory, priesthood, saint worship, mediation, affection for idols, icons and symbols… ad infinitum. We must be willing to go farther back than St. Augustine or Origen to discover the truth about Sabbath. The seventh day Sabbath is the "old way" confirmed by history, supported by the Scriptures, and boldly witnessing within us today!

Jeremiah 6:16, *"Thus saith the LORD, Stand ye in the ways, and see, and ask for the **old paths,** where is **the good way,** and walk therein, and ye shall find rest for your souls."*

5) Jesus mentioned the Sabbath as a factor at the consummation of the age.

One of the greatest proofs of the permanence of the Sabbath Day is its mention by Christ in Matthew 24:20, *"But pray ye that your flight be not in the winter, neither on the sabbath day:"*

We may speculate about the reasons *why* Messiah said this about the Sabbath Day, but one thing is clear, *IT IS A FACTOR!* The Sabbath *will*, no doubt, have some effect at the consummation of the age or He would not have mentioned it. If the Sabbath will not be a factor, if it is (or was) an insignificant or antiquated relic from historical Jewish worship, it could not be a point of concern to the last-day Believers preparing for great tribulation.

Furthermore, if the idea of Sabbath-keeping is truly of no concern to us as New Testament Believers, then of what possible consequence could it be to the Church in the last days?

Jesus mentioned it because it *is* as it always *was* – the Sabbath – the seventh day of the week – set aside as a day of rest in order to honor God and do His pleasure. A violation places us in direct opposition to this Commandment of YHVH.

6) The Sabbath is clearly witnessed by both the Law and the Prophets.

Let's take a look at the following Scriptures:

"Therefore all things whatsoever ye would that men should do to you, do ye even so to them: for this is the law and the prophets." (Matthew 7:12)

"On these two commandments hang all the law and the prophets." (Matthew 22:40)

"The law and the prophets were until John: since that time the kingdom of God is preached, and every man presseth into it." (Luke 16:16)

"Philip findeth Nathanael, and saith unto him, We have found him, of whom Moses in the law, and the prophets, did write, Jesus of Nazareth, the son of Joseph." (John 1:45)

"And after the reading of the law and the prophets...." (Acts 13:15)

"But now the righteousness of God without the law is manifested, being witnessed by the law and the prophets..." (Romans 3:21)

On the Mount of Transfiguration we see Moses and Elijah symbolizing the Law and Prophets. When Christ introduced the "Golden Rule" He gave it credibility by showing it was supported by the Law and the Prophets. The Apostle Paul argued against the accusations that he was a heretic from the standpoint that he *"...believed all things which are written in the law and in the prophets."* Can you imagine any New Testament Apostle nullifying, holding in disrepute, or setting aside the writings of the Prophets? Can you see an Apostle of Messiah saying that any one of the Laws is inapplicable or inaccurate?

It is *incomprehensible* that anyone led by the **same Spirit** who spoke and wrote through the prophets, would later deny their messages. Yet, the Law of YHVH, immutable and an inseparable brother to the Prophets, is set aside, negated, antiquated, and made into a pick and choose smorgasbord today – and no one even flinches.

Can you say, with the Apostle Paul, that YOU believe all things written in the Law and the Prophets?

7) The Sabbath will be a part of time-keeping and worship in the Kingdom of God throughout eternity.

*"For as the **new heavens and the new earth**, which I will make, shall remain before me, saith the LORD, so shall your seed and your name remain. And it shall come to pass, that **from one new moon to another, and from one sabbath to another, shall all flesh come to worship before me, saith the LORD."** (Isaiah 66:22-23)*

It is obvious that the concept of Sabbath as a sanctified day is to continue throughout eternity. It is impossible to believe that the Sabbath was for the Children of God in times past, and that it will be again in the future, but is not for us today. The *new heavens and earth* will mark the times, days, months and years just as they have from the beginning. The moon will continue to mark months and the days will continue to be counted in sevens. The Seventh Day will continue to be the same in eternity as it is now in our day – the Sabbath.

***

Summary

Historical accounts of the Sabbath can be found as early as the seventh day of creation to as late as the days of antichrist in our time. Its existence is projected well into eternity by prophecy. It should humble us to think that mankind is only a few hours older than the Sabbath and to know that the Sabbath will be here long after we are gone.

The Sabbath is a pivotal doctrine in the Scriptures. Practiced by the fathers of our faith, it is the forerunner to the disciplines of self-control and self-denial found in the New Covenant. It speaks through every gift of the Spirit, manifesting itself as rest, peace, and a meek and quiet spirit. It is a sign between our God and His people forever.

The Sabbath is neither subject to the legitimate Church, nor is it brought to heel by religious zealots creating and erasing doctrine at their own wills.

A "spiritualized" view of the Sabbath weakens the argument for keeping it as God intended and bolsters our creaturely (natural) reluctance to keep God's Commandments. To avoid hypocrisy, this view should be held and considered only as we find ourselves wholly obedient to the Commandment.

The Sabbath is remembered and kept holy by acquiescing to the vivid outlines revealed in the Scriptures. It is not subject to change or alteration in the slightest degree by anyone – nor need it be to comply and be in perfect harmony with New Testament living.

I challenge you to consider your habits, beliefs, and practices in this matter. Determine the reason you do what you do and when you do it. Be ashamed if you find that tradition or personal preference has overridden God's expressed Commandment – and do whatever it takes to change it!

In short, the Sabbath has stood as the sign between YHVH and His people (Spiritual Israel) for centuries, and it continues to stand today.

Read Exodus 31:13-18, again, as if for the first time:

> *"... Verily my sabbaths ye shall keep: for it is a sign between me and you throughout your generations; that ye may know that I am the LORD that doth sanctify you...Six days may work be done; but in the seventh is the sabbath of rest, holy to the LORD... to observe the sabbath throughout their generations, for a perpetual covenant.* **It is a sign between me and the children of Israel for ever**: *for in six days the LORD made heaven and earth, and*

on the seventh day he rested, and was refreshed. And he gave unto Moses…tables of stone, written with the finger of God."
[Whereupon He engraved…]

"Remember the Sabbath day, to keep it holy."

NOTES:

This book is available in Spanish.
Also, CD and Mp3 audio disks, and Internet
downloads are available in English and Spanish.

Order at
www.ThinkRedInk.com